WHAT DO THE LONELY DO AT CHRISTMAS

Monica Lynese Guthrie Purchase

ISBN: 979-8-9940503-0-9

Printed in the United States of America

Design & Layout: ChatGPT in collaboration with Monica Guthrie Purchase

Cover Design: Monica Guthrie Purchase

For questions, speaking engagements, or media inquiries, contact:

 JustMoniP@gmail.com or monigp1908@gmail.com

Follow Monica on social media: IG & TikTok: @monilove1908, YouTube: @TheMoniBrand

DEDICATION

In loving memory of my Godmother, Sharon Beck Crowe, my Aunt Carolyn Baker, and my Godbrother, Melvin Crispell. Your love, laughter, and legacy still live in me.

To every reader holding this book- may this be your reminder that your last lonely Christmas was your last lonely Christmas.

From this season forward, may you keep choosing joy, keep holding on to hope, and keep believing that your best days aren't behind you— they're just ahead.

ACKNOWLEDGMENTS

To my "senagers" — my parents William (Billy) and Brenda Guthrie— thank you for keeping me laughing, humble, and on my toes. You remind me that love sometimes looks like tough lessons, repeated conversations, a whole lot of grace, and raising my parents. LOL

To my children, Jalen (JT) and Josiah, and my sweet grandbaby Justice and my new grandbaby that is on the way— you are my heart walking outside of my body. You've taught me patience, purpose, and unconditional love in every season. Watching you grow has been one of the greatest blessings of my life.

To my blood brother, Corey (aka Jerkface) — thank you for being my day-one. You've loved me,bullied me(yes I still have PTSD from the bowling ball. lol), challenged me, and kept me laughing through it all. I wouldn't trade our bond (or your sarcasm) for anything.

To my chosen sisters, Tanika and Lynn — thank you for inviting me into your family and making sure I never miss another Christmas. You showed me that healing often comes through connection, laughter, and good food. You helped bring the sister circle (Kristie, Queta, Jacinta, Raquel, Kami, Sheila, and Kim) into my life. I am FOREVER grateful.

My Pastor Dr Truel D Felder, Marlene McDonald, Terry Reed, Mikey, Corey, LPT, DOJ, Fred Nelson and the whole New Faith Baptist Church International Family, thank you for being my home and filling station.

And to those who I thought broke my heart — thank you. What you really did was free me. You made room for the man, the peace, and the purpose that God actually has for me. Turns out, some heartbreaks were just heaven's way of helping me heal.

Finally, to every reader who picked up this devotional — thank you for trusting me to walk this journey with you. My prayer is that you find hope, joy, and peace in these pages, and that you remember: you are never truly alone.

With love and gratitude,

Monica Guthrie Purchase

TABLE OF CONTENTS

INTRODUCTION

What Do the Lonely Do at Christmas: A Survival Guide

Every year around the holidays, it feels like the same soundtrack is on repeat. The lights go up, the commercials start rolling, the social feeds explode with "perfect" family pictures, and then—without fail—I hear that old song: "What do the lonely do at Christmas?" (shoutout to The Emotions). And honestly? Some years I wanted to shout back at the radio, "OH, SHUT UP!" Or I wanted to cuss (and sometimes I did! Yep! I said it.)

The truth is, I didn't need a reminder that I was lonely. I already knew. And scrolling through Instagram or Facebook with all the #ThisIsUs holiday posts, surprise proposals, gift exchanges, and matching pajama photo shoots only made it worse.

For me, the ache wasn't about not having any family—I had my parents (my "senagers"), my kids, my grandbaby. It was about the empty space where I wanted a husband, a partner, someone to share these

1

moments with. And when another Christmas rolled around without that, the question of "what do the lonely do?" hit a little too close to home.

Some years, I tried to stuff it down. Other years, depression showed up like an uninvited guest, whispering lies that my story was over. I fought tears at dinners, side-eyed proposals, and spent nights wondering if things would ever change. But I also learned something: loneliness doesn't get to have the final say. God does.

This survival guide is born out of that tension. It's not fluff. It's not sugarcoated. These are real reflections from real experiences—times I've fought loneliness, depression, even thoughts of giving up—and the practical ways God, therapy, and intentional choices helped me hold on.

Each day you'll find:

- A scripture to ground you.

- A reflection that tells the truth—because healing starts with honesty.

- A meditation moment to pause, breathe, and sit with God.

- A survival tip to help you navigate the emotional weight of the season.

- A connection challenge to help you step toward community instead of isolation.

- A song of the day to lift your spirit and guide your meditation.

So whether you're single, grieving, healing, or just feeling overlooked in a season that seems to shine a spotlight on everyone else's joy, this devotional is for you. Together, we'll walk through these days—some heavy, some holy—toward hope, peace, and even joy.

Because the truth is, we already know what the lonely do at Christmas. They survive. And with God's help, they can do more than survive—they can thrive.

DAY 1 – WHEN GRATITUDE FEELS HARD

Scripture:

"Give thanks in all circumstances; for this is God's will for you in Christ Jesus."
– 1 Thessalonians 5:18

Reflection:

Gratitude sounds good in theory. It preaches easy, but it lives hard. I can't count how many nights I've sat in my room, scrolling through pictures of smiling families and couples in matching pajamas, while I felt completely unseen. My parents—my "senagers" (senior citizens who act like teenagers 🧑‍🦳♀️🧓)—were in the next room, but even with them around, the ache of being single pressed heavy on me. My children were grown and living their own lives. My granddaughter was in L.A. The house wasn't empty, but my heart often was.

That's the thing about loneliness—it magnifies what you don't have and blinds you to what's right in front of you. Depression loves to tag-team with loneliness, whispering lies like, "See? Nothing's changing. You're still here. Still alone." And if I'm honest, some years I believed it. Some years I pulled back, isolating myself because I didn't want to be around "happy" people.

But slowly, God began to shift my perspective. Gratitude wasn't a denial of how I felt—it was a weapon against despair. Gratitude said, "Yes, I feel this ache, but no, I won't let it drown out what's still good." Sometimes my gratitude list was tiny: "Thank You, Lord, that I made it through today." Other times it was specific: "Thank You for my parents' laughter. Thank You for hearing my grandbaby's voice, even if it was just through FaceTime."

Here's the truth I've learned: Gratitude doesn't erase loneliness. But it keeps loneliness from erasing me.

Meditation:

Take a deep breath. Close your eyes and picture the places in your life where gratitude feels hardest. Maybe it's the empty side of the bed. Maybe it's the seat at the table that's never filled. Maybe it's the milestone that hasn't happened yet.

Now picture Jesus sitting in that exact space with you. Not rushing you. Not scolding you for being sad. Just with you. In His presence, name three small mercies you can hold onto. Write them down. Speak them out loud. Let them become your anchors in this season.

Survival Tip – Gratitude Anchors:

1. Write down 3 specific things you're grateful for today.

2. Post them where you'll see them daily—on your mirror, fridge, or lock screen.

3. Every morning this week, read them aloud before starting your day. When loneliness whispers, answer with gratitude.

Connection Challenge:

Write your declaration and post it somewhere you'll see daily. If you're ready, share it with someone you trust—or keep it between you and God.

 "I Am Light" – India.Arie (neo-soul reminder of your worth and identity in God).

DAY 2 – WHEN THE TABLE FEELS DIFFERENT

Scripture:

" You prepare a table before me in the presence of my enemies."
– Psalm 23:5

Reflection:

Holiday tables tell stories—and not always the ones we expect. Mine has never been empty, but it hasn't always been full either. I live with my parents—my "senagers," who keep me laughing and rolling my eyes at the same time. My oldest child might drop in, but my youngest lives out of state, and my granddaughter has never been at our holiday table because she lives in L.A.

So the table is set. The food is cooked. But if I'm honest, sometimes my heart still feels the emptiness of who isn't there. For years, I dreamed of something bigger: a home full of people, laughter spilling out of the kitchen, kids running everywhere, music playing, and me hosting like the leading lady in a holiday movie. And let's be real—I give leading lady energy.

Don't play with me, Hallmark, I could carry the whole film!

But that hasn't been my story—at least not yet. And that gap—the one between my desire and my reality—has sometimes made the holidays heavy.

Here's what I've learned: God still prepares tables. Sometimes they're not the ones we imagined. Sometimes they're smaller, quieter, even messier. But His presence at the table makes it holy. It reminds me that love is still present, even if it looks different than what I longed for.

So when I sit at a table that feels too quiet, I've started to shift my view. Instead of only seeing who's missing, I choose to notice who is there. And I remind myself that one day, I may sit at the table I've dreamed of—but until then, I'm still being fed by God's love right here.

Meditation:

Close your eyes and picture your holiday table. Who's there? Who isn't? Be honest about how that makes you feel. Don't rush past the ache—bring it before God. Now picture Jesus seated at the table with you. His presence fills every empty seat. Whisper this prayer: "Lord, thank You for this table today. Teach me to see Your presence in what I have, even while I trust You with what I long for."

Survival Tip – The Table Exercise:

1. Write out a description of your dream table—what it would look like, sound like, feel like. Be specific.

2. Then write down one thing you're grateful for about the table you do have today.

3. Place both lists somewhere you can return to. Let one fuel your prayers and the other fuel your gratitude.

Connection Challenge:

Take a picture of your table this season. If it feels safe, share it with someone you trust. If not, save it as a reminder that God met you there too.

🎵 "Do You Hear What I Hear?" – Whitney Houston (a Christmas classic reminding us the true Guest of honor is always present).

DAY 3 – WHEN COMPARISON CREEPS IN

Scripture:

"*Each one should test their own actions. Then they can take pride in themselves alone, without comparing themselves to someone else.*"
– Galatians 6:4

Reflection:

If the holidays had a sport, it would be called The Comparison Games. And let me tell you, I used to play it like it was the Olympics. Scrolling through Instagram and Facebook, seeing families in their matching pajamas, couples under the mistletoe, surprise proposals, and gift exchanges that looked straight out of a Hallmark movie—it stung.

I'd sit there thinking, "Lord, why not me? When is it my turn?" And then I'd spiral: another Christmas alone, another birthday alone, another New Year's Eve without a midnight kiss. Comparison magnifies what you don't have until it drowns out what you do.

And here's the kicker: I did have blessings. I had my "senagers" keeping me laughing, my kids, my grandbaby in L.A., friends who had become family. But comparison made me feel like all of that wasn't enough—like my life didn't measure up because it didn't look like theirs.

Here's the truth: comparison is a thief. It robs you of joy and blinds you to your own gifts. It took therapy, prayer, and a whole lot of tears for me to learn that someone else's timeline isn't my timeline. Their highlight reel doesn't cancel out my story. And listen—don't let Instagram fool you. Half the couples in those matching pajamas were probably arguing before the camera clicked.

God isn't waiting for me to "catch up" with someone else. He's writing my story on His timeline. And if He hasn't given it yet, it's not because He forgot—it's because He's not done.

Meditation:

Take a breath and think about the last time comparison crept in. What triggered it? A picture? A post? A conversation? Be honest about how it made you feel. Now bring that moment to God. Whisper this prayer: "Lord, help me see my life through Your eyes, not through someone else's filter. Teach me to value what You've already given me."

Survival Tip – Reclaim Your Joy List:

1. Write down 5 blessings in your life that you wouldn't trade for anything—not even matching pajamas.

2. Keep that list somewhere close (in your journal, on your phone, or in your Bible).

3. The next time comparison creeps in, stop scrolling, read that list out loud, and thank God for each one.

Connection Challenge:

Buy yourself a small gift. If you're comfortable, snap a pic and share it as a declaration that you are worth celebrating. Or simply unwrap it privately and thank God for the gift of you.

🎵 "Be Blessed" – Yolanda Adams (a gospel/R&B anthem affirming God's blessings for others don't cancel yours).

DAY 4 – WHEN YOU'RE CLINGING TO HOPE

Scripture:

" The virgin will conceive and give birth to a son, and they will call him Immanuel (which means 'God with us')."
– Matthew 1:23

Reflection:

Hope feels easy to preach but hard to practice— especially around the holidays. My birthday is on New Year's Eve, so the season hits me double. I'd look at the calendar and think, another Christmas alone, another birthday alone, another year without the love I've been praying for. The weight of it pressed so heavy some years that depression showed up like an uninvited guest. There were moments when suicidal thoughts tried to take me out.

But in those moments, God's whisper cut through the darkness: "Your story isn't over." Sometimes I felt Him so close it was like He was rocking me in His arms, reminding me, "I see you. I love you. You are not forgotten."

That's what hope looked like for me—not a loud declaration or a lightning-bolt miracle. Sometimes hope was as small as choosing to get out of bed. Sometimes it was holding onto a scripture when nothing in my life matched it. Sometimes it was showing up to therapy, tears and all, and letting someone remind me I still had a future.

Immanuel means "God with us." That's not just a Christmas story—it's a survival story. Because when everything in me wanted to quit, the truth that He was with me kept me breathing, kept me waiting, kept me alive.

Meditation:

Pause. Close your eyes. Picture the area of your life where hope feels fragile—where the waiting is longest. What does it look like? What does it feel like? Now picture Jesus standing in that very place with you. Hear Him say: "I am with you. Your story is not over." Whisper this prayer: "Lord, even when my hope feels small, help me hold on to the truth that You are with me."

Survival Tip – Anchor Your Hope:

1. Light a candle today as a symbol of hope.

2. Write down one thing you're still daring to believe God for, even if it feels impossible.

3. Place it near the candle. Each day this week, relight the candle and pray over that one hope.

Connection Challenge:

Tell one safe person what you're still hoping for. If you're not ready, write it as a prayer in your journal and invite God to touch and agree with you.

▌ "Heaven Help Us All" – Stevie Wonder (soulful honesty about brokenness while clinging to divine hope).

DAY 5 – WHEN YOU NEED TO BUILD CONNECTION

Scripture:

"*Two are better than one, because they have a good return for their labor: if either of them falls down, one can help the other up.*"
– Ecclesiastes 4:9–10

Reflection:

Loneliness will always tell you to isolate. It whispers, "Stay home. Don't bother people. Nobody cares anyway." And the more you listen, the heavier the silence gets. I've been there—closing myself off, convincing myself it was better not to show up at all. But the truth is, healing doesn't happen in isolation. Healing happens in connection.

My family has always been there for me, but God also placed people in my life like Tanika and Lynn—women who embraced me as their own. They didn't just invite me into their homes, they invited me into their lives. And they gave me something I didn't even realize I needed: a safe place to belong.

Building connection doesn't mean you have to be the life of the party or fill your calendar with events. Sometimes it's as simple as saying "yes" to a coffee invitation. Sometimes it's texting a friend and saying, "Hey, I could use some company today." And sometimes it's creating your own tradition—like buying yourself a gift, journaling, or even planning a birthday trip.

Even Jesus didn't walk alone. He surrounded Himself with people, even though they weren't perfect. If He needed community, so do we.

Meditation:

Think about the last time you felt truly seen, heard, or cared for by someone. What did that moment feel like? Let yourself sit with the memory. Thank God for that person. Whisper this prayer: "Lord, remind me that I don't have to carry life alone. Show me who I can reach out to, and teach me how to let people in."

Survival Tip – Build Your Connection Plan:

1. Write down 3–5 safe people you can lean on in this season.

2. Circle one person's name and reach out today with a simple text: "Hey, would you be open to coffee / a call / catching up this week?"

3. Repeat this once a week during the season. Pre-plan lifelines so loneliness doesn't sneak up and take over.

Connection Challenge:

Journal about a time someone showed up for you. If you feel led, send them a thank-you message. Or simply pray for them in gratitude if sharing feels too vulnerable.

🎵 "Better Than You Left Me" – Mickey Guyton (country soul about resilience, reminding you connection heals and strengthens).

DAY 6 – WHEN TRIGGERS CATCH YOU OFF GUARD

Scripture:

> "*Rejoice with those who rejoice; mourn with those who mourn.*"
> – Romans 12:15

Reflection:

Let me be honest—matching pajamas are a trigger for me. And listen, I love pajamas. I've got cute ones, cozy ones, festive ones—even pink and green sorority ones (because you know I rep my AKA). But every time I see those family photos or couples' selfies in their coordinated sets, my heart takes a hit. It's not really about the pajamas—it's about what they represent: connection, intimacy, belonging.

And the truth is, I want that too. I want someone to laugh with while we unwrap gifts in silly flannel pants. I want to wake up on Christmas morning and know there's someone next to me. Seeing others have it sometimes feels like salt in a wound.

For a long time, I felt guilty for admitting that. I thought maybe I wasn't "spiritual enough" if I couldn't just be happy for other people. But God reminded me—it's okay to grieve what you don't have while still rejoicing for what others do. Both can be true.

The key is not letting the trigger spiral into despair. Instead of scrolling and sinking, I've learned to pause and pray: "Lord, You see the desires of my heart. Help me wait with hope, not bitterness."

Meditation:

Pause for a moment and think about your triggers—the things that catch you off guard and stir up loneliness. Be honest about them. Now imagine handing them to God, one by one, like wrapped gifts. Whisper this prayer: "Lord, I give You the triggers that hurt me. Teach me how to see them as reminders to turn back to You."

Survival Tip – Flip the Trigger:

1. Identify one holiday trigger that hits you hardest (photos, commercials, events).

2. When it shows up, pause and name it out loud: "This hurts because I long for it too."

3. Then flip it into a prayer: "God, I trust You with this desire. Teach me to hope without bitterness."

Connection Challenge:

Create your own joy moment. If you want, take a picture and share it. Or keep it private as a reminder that you are worth celebrating.

🎵 "Someday at Christmas" – Stevie Wonder (a Christmas ballad pointing to hope beyond what we see).

DAY 7 – WHEN YOU DON'T WANT TO SHOW UP

Scripture:

"I will never leave you nor forsake you."
– Hebrews 13:5

Reflection:

There have been times I've pulled up to an event, sat in the car, and then pulled right back out without even going in. The makeup was done, the outfit was cute, lashes were holding on for dear life—but my heart just couldn't do it. I told myself, "I'll go next time." But next time didn't always come.

Holiday parties are supposed to be fun—but for me, they've sometimes felt like the loneliest rooms in the world. I'd walk in smiling, plate in hand, trying to blend in, but inside I was thinking, "Everybody else has someone. And me? I'm just here...again." Then, like clockwork, someone would pat my shoulder and say, "Don't worry, sis. He's on his way." And I'd want to yell, "Well, can I get a tracking number? Because he is taking his sweet time finding me!"

Some years, I laughed, sang, danced, and showed up in full "life of the party" mode—yet nobody knew how lonely I was inside. I'd smile for pictures and go home to silence. I'd post joyful photos while silently crying in the dark, wondering if anyone could see past the light I was trying so hard to keep shining.

But then came the year I said yes to my chosen sister Lynn's invitation. I didn't want to go, but something in me knew I needed to—plus she threatened me and told me I better not miss another Christmas! ▌ When I walked into her house, I felt something different— genuine love. No pretense, no pity, no reminders of what I didn't have. Just warmth, laughter, and real connection. Her entire family embraced me like I'd always been part of them.

As we added items to the family's Christmas time capsule, they laughed and said, "You know you're officially family now—you're stuck with us!" That night healed something in me. It reminded me that God will send people to fill spaces you thought would always stay empty.

I realized that sometimes, showing up isn't about me at all—it's about who God wants to reach through me. I may not leave holding someone's hand, but I never leave empty-handed. God fills the space where loneliness tries to sit.

Even on the nights I feel invisible, He still sees me. Even when I feel forgotten, He still whispers, "You're mine." And even when I want to stay home, He reminds me that when I walk into a room, I don't walk in alone.

Meditation:

Think of a time you didn't want to show up but pushed yourself anyway.

How did you feel before, during, and after?

Whisper this prayer:

> "Lord, teach me to measure my moments by Your presence, not my status.
> Remind me that when I walk in a room, I never walk in alone."

Survival Tip – Redefine the Win:

1. If you go to a gathering, set one simple goal: meet one new person or have one meaningful conversation.

2. If you choose to stay home, don't sit in isolation—plan an alternative joy moment. Watch your favorite movie, FaceTime someone safe, or cook yourself a meal you love.

3. Remember: showing up isn't about proving anything—it's about honoring your needs and protecting your peace.

Connection Challenge:

After an event, call or text a friend who makes you feel safe and grounded. If you're not up to talking, write down one highlight or "heart moment" from the evening—something that reminded you of God's faithfulness—so the night doesn't end with heaviness.

🎙 Song of the Day:

"You Know My Name" – Tasha Cobbs Leonard (feat. Jimi Cravity)

A soul-stirring reminder that you are never unseen or forgotten. Even when you feel invisible in a crowded room or weary from showing up with a heavy heart, God still knows your name, your story, and your struggle. This song declares His intimate presence —

that He walks beside you, covers you, and calls you His own. Let it wash over you as you remember: you never walk in alone.

What Do Lonely Do At Christmas

DAY 8 – WHEN THE EMPTY CHAIR FEELS TOO LOUD

Scripture:

"*He heals the brokenhearted and binds up their wounds.*"
– Psalm 147:3

Reflection:

Holiday tables always tell the truth. For some, the chair that's empty is the one where a loved one used to sit. For others, it's the absence of a spouse, a child, or a dream unfulfilled. I've felt both—the grief of loss and the sting of longing.

It's those quiet moments—the extra plate not set, the laugh not heard—that can undo you. I've had holidays where the tears fell into my plate before the meal was even served. I've had others where my temper was short because sadness had been sitting with me all day.

Luther Vandross sang it best in "A House Is Not a Home": "A chair is still a chair, even when there's no one sitting there." And isn't that the truth? The chair itself doesn't change—but the absence of who should be there makes it deafening. Sometimes it feels like the chair is mocking you: "See? Still empty. Still waiting."

But here's the comfort: God doesn't walk past the empty chair. He sits with us in the silence. He binds wounds, not with clichés, but with His presence. And sometimes His comfort shows up through unexpected touches—a friend's last-minute invite, a memory that makes you laugh before it makes you cry, or the Spirit whispering, "You're not forgotten."

Meditation:

Picture the chair that feels empty for you. Whose absence does it represent? Let the ache rise to the surface. Don't rush past it. Now picture Jesus sitting in that chair—not as a replacement, but as a presence. Whisper this prayer: "Lord, I give You the ache of my empty places. Fill them with Your love."

Survival Tip – Acknowledge the Chair:

1. Write down one memory of the person or one prayer about the longing.

2. Place it in an envelope, ornament, or keepsake box.

3. When the ache rises, revisit it and invite God into that moment.

Connection Challenge:

Tell someone safe about the chair that feels loud. If you're not ready to share, write it in your journal and invite God into that ache.

🎵 "A House Is Not a Home" – Luther Vandross (soulful R&B capturing the ache of absence, paired with God's comfort).

DAY 9 – WHEN WEARINESS SETS IN

Scripture:

"Even youths grow tired and weary, and young men stumble and fall; but those who hope in the Lord will renew their strength."
– Isaiah 40:30–31

Reflection:

There was a time in my life when weariness wasn't just emotional — it was spiritual. I was in my marriage, trying to hold it all together on the outside, but inside I was falling apart. I was exhausted from pretending things were okay when they weren't. I was tired of smiling in public and crying in private.

I'd show up for everyone else — church, work, my kids — but when I came home, the silence was deafening. The kind of silence that makes you question if your life even matters. I was at an all-time low. The pain felt unending, the disappointment unbearable, and the loneliness crippling.

I remember one night crying out to God, broken, empty, and ready to give up. I didn't see a way forward. I didn't think I could take another day of the same. But even in that dark space, something small — almost like a whisper — stirred in me. I picked up a pen. And the words that came out weren't from my head. They poured straight from my soul.

That's the night "Anointing Fall" was born — the first song I ever wrote. It wasn't just a song; it was my lifeline. Every lyric carried a piece of my surrender:

> "Here we are alone, it's just You and I...
> I don't have to be afraid, every tear I cry, You will dry..."

Through that song, God reminded me that He was still there — even when I didn't feel Him. He was holding me through my hurt, waiting for me to release what I'd been trying to carry alone. That song became my prayer. It washed over my pain, broke through my despair, and reminded me that His anointing still flowed over broken things — even me.

So now, when weariness creeps in — when life feels heavy and joy feels distant — I remember that night. I remember how close God was to me in the darkness.

Renewal didn't come with a bang; it came with a whisper and a melody.

God didn't just save me from that night — He birthed something through it. And that's what I want you to hold on to: your weary place can still be the birthplace of something beautiful.

Meditation:

Close your eyes and take a deep breath.

Where do you feel the heaviness — in your body, your mind, your heart?

Picture yourself laying that weariness down at Jesus' feet.

Whisper this prayer:

> "Lord, I am tired, but my hope is in You.
> I may not have the strength to keep going on my own,
> but You said You would renew me.
> Let Your anointing fall fresh on me again."

Survival Tip – Practice Renewal:

1. Schedule one intentional rest moment this week — nap, journal, stretch, sit in stillness, or just breathe.

2. Write down one scripture that breathes life into you (start with Isaiah 40:31) and keep it somewhere visible.

3. Every time weariness whispers, stop and read it out loud. Let His Word recharge you before the world drains you.

Connection Challenge:

Reach out to someone you trust and simply say, "I'm tired." You don't have to explain it or fix it — just let yourself be known. If that feels too hard, journal your truth and pray over it. God meets us in honesty more than perfection.

Song: "Anointing Fall" – Monica Purchase

A testimony turned into melody — a song birthed in brokenness that became a reminder of God's power to restore.

Monica Lynese Guthrie Purchase

DAY 10 – WHEN JOY FEELS SMALL

Scripture:

" *The joy of the Lord is your strength.* "
– Nehemiah 8:10

Reflection:

There were years when joy felt like it belonged to other people—the ones with picture-perfect families, matching pajamas, surprise proposals, and Christmas cards full of smiles. Meanwhile, I was just trying to breathe, praying I didn't burst into tears while scrolling through another "perfect" holiday post.

I remember one year in particular when I was worn out mentally and emotionally. I showed up for everyone else—the church program, the service, the family event—smiling, singing, and serving like everything was fine. But when I got home, the silence was deafening. The house was still, and so was my spirit. I remember sitting down with my journal, tears in my eyes, and whispering, "Lord, I'm trying. I really am."

Joy felt small that year. But even in that stillness, God reminded me—His joy isn't about everything being right. It's about Him being present when things aren't.

Over time, I've learned that joy often shows up in quiet, simple ways:

- Laughing so hard with my sisters that my face hurt.

- Hearing my grandbaby Justice—who calls me Momo—yell "MO-MOOOO!" through FaceTime like it was the best part of her day.

- Admiring the fresh fallen snow out the window, while also being a little mad that I had to shovel it. (Balance, y'all. ▌)

- Sitting down with my journal, reflecting on His goodness, even when my emotions were slow to catch up.

Those were my small joys. Not flashy. Not filtered. Just real.

And each one reminded me that joy doesn't skip us— it sometimes just sneaks in quietly, disguised as gratitude, laughter, or a sacred pause.

The joy of the Lord is my strength, not because it cancels out pain, but because it carries me through it.

Meditation:

Take a deep breath and think about one small joy that found you this week.

It doesn't have to be big—it just has to be real.

Now whisper this prayer:

> "Lord, thank You for the joy that strengthens me, even when it comes in small, quiet ways.
> Help me see You in the laughter, in the stillness, and even in the snow.
> Teach me to hold onto joy, because it holds onto me."

Survival Tip – Cultivate Joy:

1. Do one intentional thing today that makes you smile—call a loved one, make a comfort meal, or take a slow drive with your favorite playlist.

2. Start a Joy Journal. Each day, jot down one thing that brought you peace or laughter.

3. When the season feels heavy, read through that list and let it remind you—God's joy never ran out; it's just been waiting for you to notice it again.

Connection Challenge:

Text or call someone who always makes you laugh. If that feels like too much today, that's okay—write your moment of joy down privately and thank God for it. Joy grows when you give it space to breathe.

▎ Song of the Day – "This Christmas" by Donny Hathaway

A soulful reminder that joy doesn't have to be loud to be powerful. Let the music fill your space and remind you that joy can live in reflection, in laughter, and even in the quiet moments you share with God.

DAY 11 – WHEN CHURCH FEELS HEAVY

Scripture:

*"Come to me, all you who are weary and burdened,
and I will give you rest."*
– Matthew 11:28

Reflection:

Let's just be honest—church during the holidays can be a lot. Between the Christmas concerts, extra rehearsals, and people asking if you can "just hit that one part again," sometimes I've wanted to say, "I love Jesus, but y'all... I'm tired."

And while it's supposed to be the most joyful time of year, there are moments I've walked in smiling on the outside but feeling heavy on the inside. The weight of waiting, disappointment, or just plain emotional fatigue can make even worship feel like work.

I remember one particular year someone slid in my DMs talking about how much they admired my faith, my smile, my "energy." It all started out so sweet. I thought, okay Lord, maybe this is my year. Maybe this is finally the connection I've prayed for. But right before Christmas, he completely ghosted me. I had to call him myself just to find out what was going on, and he had the nerve to blame it on his dog. 🐕 I promise, I can't make this up—sometimes my life feels like a sad sitcom. 😔

Still, even after that disappointment, I showed up. I kept serving. I kept singing. I kept doing what I knew to do—because that's what faith taught me. But no lie, I had my days. I was frustrated. I didn't understand. I asked God, "Why does it keep feeling like this? Why does it seem so easy for everyone else?"

But here's what He showed me: even when I don't understand, He's still consistent. People might disappear, but He doesn't. When my hope feels bruised, His love doesn't change.

That year, I learned that God isn't moved by my performance—He's moved by my presence. He doesn't need me to be perfect or upbeat. He just wants the real me—the weary, confused, "trying my best not to cry through rehearsal" me. Because He can handle that version too.

Now, when I show up to church tired, I show up honest. I let Him meet me in the middle of the mess. Because worship isn't about pretending you're fine— it's about trusting that He's still good, even when life feels unfair.

Meditation:

Before you walk into church this week, pause in your car. Take a breath and say, "Lord, I'm here. I may be tired, but I'm here."

Then imagine Him smiling and saying:

> "You don't have to earn My presence.
> You don't have to fake your strength.
> I'm already here, waiting to meet you."

Survival Tip – Release the Pressure:

1. Identify one way you've been "pushing through" on empty—smiling, serving, or pretending you're fine.

2. Choose one way this week to be honest about where you are—maybe by resting, journaling, or asking for help.

3. Give yourself grace. Showing up tired is still showing up.

Connection Challenge:

If you feel safe, text or call someone from church and say, "Hey sis/bro, I'm showing up, but I'm a little heavy this week."

If that feels like too much, write it in your journal. Let your honesty become your offering.

Song of the Day – "My Worship" by Phil Thompson

A gentle reminder that worship isn't about perfection—it's about surrender. Even when your energy is low and your joy feels small, God still calls what you bring beautiful.

Monica Lynese Guthrie Purchase

DAY 12 – WHEN FINANCES FEEL TIGHT

Scripture:

"*And my God will meet all your needs according to the riches of his glory in Christ Jesus.*"
– Philippians 4:19

Reflection:

Whew... let's talk about it. The holidays have a way of trying to make you feel like your worth is tied to your wallet. Every commercial, every "gift guide," every "must-have" post is out here whispering, "Buy this if you really care." Meanwhile, I'm sitting at home thinking, "My care and my coins are not in agreement right now."

I've had seasons where my budget didn't stretch as far as my heart wanted it to. Where I wanted to do all the things—buy the gifts, travel, host the dinner—but my bank account was like, "Ma'am, sit down." And in those moments, shame tried to creep in. That little voice that said, "You're not doing enough."

But God had to remind me—love isn't measured in money. Peace is worth more than debt. And joy? Joy has never been for sale.

Some of my most meaningful Christmases didn't include fancy gifts or extravagant dinners. They were the years I sat around the table laughing with my family, or dropped off cookies to a neighbor, or gave my time when I couldn't give much else.

I've seen God stretch a dollar, multiply leftovers, and send unexpected blessings that met needs I never even voiced out loud.

And can I be honest? There's a freedom in not trying to keep up. You realize that the people who love you, love you—not the presents, not the wrapping paper, not the "look what I got" moment.

So if this is one of those lean years, breathe. You're not behind. You're not less than. You're human. And your presence—the laughter, the love, the way you show up—is still a gift.

Meditation:

Think of a time when your money was funny, but God still made a way.

Now whisper this prayer:

> "Lord, free me from the pressure to perform with money.
> Teach me to value peace over purchases and memories over material things.
> Remind me that my worth isn't in what I can buy, but in who I am in You."

Survival Tip – Simplicity Over Shame:

1. Set a boundary your budget can handle and stick to it. (And if anyone calls you cheap, tell them you're walking in wisdom. 🙂)

2. Write down three creative, non-monetary ways to show love this season—like handwritten notes, cooking a meal, or offering a helping hand.

3. Repeat this truth: "I am enough, even without excess."

Connection Challenge:

Share a simple joy with someone—a moment that reminded you love isn't about price tags. Maybe it was a meal shared, a laugh exchanged, or peace in your own quiet space.

If you're not ready to share, journal it as a reminder that joy can't be bought—but it can always be found.

▍Song of the Day – "Silver & Gold" by Kirk Franklin

This one says it all: "I'd rather have Jesus than silver and gold."

Let it wash over you as a reminder that your true wealth isn't in your account balance—it's in His faithfulness, your peace, and the love that money could never buy.

DAY 13 – WHEN CONDEMNATION CREEPS IN

Scripture:

"I have learned to be content whatever the circumstances."
– Philippians 4:11

Reflection:

Whew, this one hits home. For years, I used to beat myself up for wanting more. I'd sit there thinking, "If I were really grateful, I wouldn't feel lonely. I wouldn't want a husband so bad. I wouldn't be scrolling Pinterest looking at 'wedding inspiration' boards for a man who doesn't even exist yet."

And that's just like that ole sapsucka Satan — always twisting the truth just enough to make you doubt your own heart. He knows he can't take your faith, so he tries to drain your joy by whispering, "You're not content enough. You're failing at faith."

For a long time, I believed that lie. I thought my desire meant I was doing this "whole faith walk" wrong.

But then I realized something — Paul said he learned to be content. He didn't wake up one morning after prayer and coffee suddenly zen and satisfied. No, he learned it. That means it took time, tears, therapy, and a whole lot of trust.

Contentment isn't pretending you don't want what you want. You can love God, be grateful, serve, sing, shout, tithe, and still desire companionship, consistency, or even a different season of life. Wanting more doesn't make you ungrateful — it makes you human.

I remember one night, I was journaling and finally got honest with God. I wrote, "Lord, I love You, but I'm struggling. I'm grateful for everything You've done, but this part of my heart still aches."

And I'll never forget the peace that washed over me as I felt Him whisper, "I'm not mad at you for that. I planted that desire. You don't have to hide it from Me."

Because that's what He wants — honesty. Psalm 51:6 says, "Behold, You desire truth in the inward parts." God doesn't want our polished prayers; He wants our whole hearts. He wants us to come to Him raw, messy, uncertain, and real. Because healing can't start in hiding.

That changed everything.

God never condemns you for your ache. He simply invites you to bring both your gratitude and your longing to Him. You can hold joy in one hand and hope in the other — and neither cancels the other out.

Meditation:

Close your eyes and think of something you've wanted but felt guilty for desiring.

Now whisper this prayer:

> "Lord, I give You my longing.
> Teach me to hold gratitude and hope together without shame.
> Remind me that I'm not failing for wanting more — I'm learning how to trust You in the wait.
> Thank You for loving the honest version of me."

Survival Tip – Gratitude + Desire:

1. Write down one thing you're longing for — something your heart still hopes for.

2. Write down one thing you're grateful for today — proof of His goodness.

3. Pray over both lists. Let gratitude anchor you while hope keeps your heart open.

Connection Challenge:

If you feel ready, share with someone safe:

> "I'm grateful, but I still long for ___."
> If that feels too personal, write it privately. God can hold both your tears and your dreams at the same time.

▮ Song of the Day – "Be Grateful" by Walter Hawkins

Let this classic remind you: your gratitude doesn't cancel your desire, and your desire doesn't disqualify your faith. You can be grateful and expectant — God honors both.

Monica Lynese Guthrie Purchase

DAY 14 – WHEN MUSIC TRIGGERS MEMORIES

Scripture:

"*Sing to the Lord a new song, for He has done marvelous things.*"
– Psalm 98:1

Reflection:

Whew — music can be a whole experience! One second you're fine, the next a Christmas song comes on, and suddenly you're fighting back tears in the middle of the grocery store like, "Lord, not 'This Christmas' again!" ⏸

Music is powerful. It carries memories you didn't ask for — the relationship that ended, the one that never really began, the moment you thought it was finally your turn. I've had songs that hit before the first chorus, not because the notes were wrong but because the memory was loud.

And listen, I love music — shoot, I am music. ⏸ I've got a song for everything! If I can't find one that fits, I'll make one up on the spot. Music is how I pray, how I praise, and sometimes how I process. It's part of who God made me to be.

But I've learned something over the years — you've got to protect your peace, even through your playlist. There were seasons I let certain songs keep me stuck, reliving heartbreak on repeat. Now, I'm more intentional about what I allow to play in my spirit.

And listen, I've also learned I can't play Tank and stay saved and single. ▌Some songs hit way too close to what I'm trying to leave behind! Guarding my peace sometimes means changing the playlist before my emotions start singing backup.

One Christmas, I was driving home from rehearsal, and "Have Yourself a Merry Little Christmas" came on. Whew, child... I had to pull over. Between the twinkling lights and that line "through the years we all will be together" — I lost it. But here's what God whispered right there in my tear-filled Toyota:

> "You can't heal if you keep replaying the hurt. Let Me give you a new song."

And He did. Now I curate my soundtrack like my peace depends on it — because sometimes it does. I replaced my heartbreak playlist with healing music, swapped sad love songs for worship, and started letting melodies minister instead of trigger. Healing sometimes starts with changing the song.

Meditation:

Think of a song that stirs pain for you. Name it honestly. Now, think of a song that lifts you — the one that reminds you you're still standing.

Whisper this prayer:

> "Lord, help me choose melodies that draw me closer to You.
> Turn my tears into testimony,
> and teach my heart to sing again."

Survival Tip – Curate Your Soundtrack:

1. List 2 "trigger songs" to set aside for now (yes, even that one you swear you're over).

2. List 3 songs that bring peace or hope.

3. Build a playlist you can reach for when heaviness creeps in — and title it something like "Waitin' Well Vibes."

Connection Challenge:

Share one uplifting song with a friend or post it online to bless someone else. If you're not ready to share, keep it as your lifeline — a soundtrack for your survival and your praise.

▌Song of the Day – "Brighter Day" by Kirk Franklin

A burst of joy and hope that reminds you even after the tears, there's still light ahead. Kirk's declaration of faith and energy will lift your spirit and shift your atmosphere — because no matter how heavy life feels, God still has a brighter day waiting for you.

DAY 15 – WHEN SERVING BRINGS HEALING

Scripture:

"*Truly I tell you, whatever you did for one of the least of these brothers and sisters of mine, you did for me.*"
– Matthew 25:40

Reflection:

There's something about serving that has a way of putting life back in perspective. When I'm deep in my feelings — and trust me, I've been there — God always reminds me that somebody else could use a little light, too.

Some of my heaviest holidays started to lighten when I chose to give instead of grieve. The year I helped with our church's Angel Tree gift delivery, I remember looking at the names on the tags — children with incarcerated parents. Just knowing that a child who might have felt forgotten would wake up to love shown by complete strangers... it broke me in the best way. I thought, "Lord, even in the middle of pain, You still find ways to show people they're seen."

Serving has also connected me to people I might never have met otherwise. Whether it's working alongside my sorors of Alpha Kappa Alpha Sorority, Incorporated to bless families in need, volunteering through community drives, or simply encouraging someone walking through their own "silent season," I've learned that pouring into others helps refill me, too.

But let me be real — I haven't always felt like serving. There were days I showed up still frustrated, still lonely, still asking God, "Why does my table always feel half-empty?" Yet, somewhere between handing out gifts, singing at church, or showing up for someone else, my perspective shifted. I realized I wasn't just showing up for them — God was showing up for me.

That's how gentle His healing can be. He'll use your hands to bless someone else while quietly mending your heart. Serving doesn't erase the ache, but it shifts the weight. It reminds you that you're not the only one walking through hard seasons — and somehow, that realization makes room for peace again.

Meditation:

Picture yourself giving love to someone in need — a smile, a prayer, a helping hand. See their gratitude. Feel the lightness it gives you, too.

Whisper this prayer:

> "Lord, make me a vessel.
> Use my life to bring healing to others,
> even as You heal me."

Survival Tip – Plan to Serve:

1. Choose one way to serve this season — big or small. Maybe join your sorority, ministry, or community outreach in blessing a family.

2. Put it on your calendar so it becomes a commitment, not just an idea.

3. Afterward, reflect on how it shifted your heart — not just for them, but for you.

Connection Challenge:

If you feel comfortable, invite someone to serve alongside you. Healing multiplies when it's shared. If you're not ready, write about the experience and

thank God for the chance to give from your heart —
even if it's still healing.

▌ Song of the Day – "Love's In Need of Love Today" by Stevie Wonder

A timeless reminder that the world — and our hearts
— always need more love. When you give from a
sincere place, you're not just blessing others; you're
letting love heal you too.

Monica Lynese Guthrie Purchase

DAY 16 – WHEN PATTERNS STING (THE GOOD LUCK CHUCK CHRISTMAS)

Scripture:

" The Lord is close to the brokenhearted and saves those who are crushed in spirit."
– Psalm 34:18

Reflection:

There's hurt that cuts deep, and then there's hurt that feels like it's on repeat.

Remember "Dog Boy" from Day 11? Well... here's the sequel no one asked for.

I'll never forget the day I was getting ready for a Christmas concert—dressed, rehearsed, hair laid, spirit trying to be right. I was scrolling Facebook when a post stopped me cold. There he was—the same man who had pursued me heavy, love-bombed me, and then pulled back with the excuse of his old, blind dog (HIS BLIND DOG, Y'ALL!)—standing next to a bride. Married. Not years later. Months.

Now let me be clear: it wasn't about him. No shade, but I didn't care that deeply about him. What broke me was the pattern. Because truth be told, this wasn't the first time a man had love-bombed me, disappeared, and then turned around and married the next woman. At that point, it was starting to feel like my love life was sponsored by reruns.

It felt like that old movie Good Luck Chuck, where every woman a man dates marries the very next person after him. Only in my version, I was Chuck. I remember staring at the screen thinking, "Lord, am I stuck in that storyline? Am I just the training ground? The before?"

That night, I had to make an emergency call to my therapist—not because my heart was broken over a man, but because I was heartbroken over what it seemed to mean. Another reminder of not being chosen. Another Christmas with questions. Another year wrestling with worth.

But right there, in my tears, God whispered:

> "You are not overlooked. You are not disposable. Their choices don't define your value. I see you, and I will not pass you over."

Sometimes the sting of patterns makes you feel cursed—but God reminded me, broken hearts are where He draws close. The pattern wasn't punishment; it was preparation. Every "not yet" was clearing space for the man, the peace, and the purpose that would actually fit me.

Now when I think about "Dog Boy" and the rest of the Good Luck Chuck Chronicles, I laugh, shake my head, and thank God for the closed doors. Because healing means learning to stop rehearsing rejection and start recognizing redirection.

Meditation:

Think of a time you felt overlooked or replaced. Don't downplay it—name the sting. Now picture Jesus leaning close, saying: "I see you. You are not forgotten." Whisper: "Lord, heal the sting of these patterns and remind me I am chosen by You."

Survival Tip – Break the Lie:

1. Write down the lie the pattern made you believe ("I'm always the one before," "I'm not enough").

2. Next to it, write God's truth ("I am chosen," "I am worth love," "I am not forgotten").

3. Say His truth out loud until it feels louder than the lie.

Connection Challenge:

If you feel comfortable, share with a trusted friend: "I've been battling feelings of being overlooked, but I'm choosing to believe I'm still worthy of God's best." If not, write it as a private declaration in your journal.

🎵 Song of the Day: "Not Gon' Cry" – Mary J. Blige.

Because sometimes survival starts with letting the tears fall and refusing to let the pain have the final word.

What Do Lonely Do At Christmas

DAY 17 – WHEN REJECTION HITS DIFFERENT

Scripture:

"*See, I have engraved you on the palms of my hands.*"
– Isaiah 49:16

Reflection:

Rejection around the holidays? Whew. It hits different. It's not just about someone saying no — it's about the timing. The "Merry Christmas to us" couples' posts. The matching pajama photo shoots. The "she said yes!" videos that somehow always pop up right when you're eating your second slice of sweet potato pie in peace.

And here you are — just trying to stay in the spirit, but also wondering, "Lord, is it me? Am I not pretty enough? Fun enough? Spiritual enough? Why do they choose her and not me?"

I've been there. More than once. There have been times when I thought this was finally the one — he prayed, quoted scripture, maybe even sang a little. And then, out of nowhere, poof. Gone faster than my patience at the DMV. Then six months later? Married. ▌ I was like, "Okay, Lord, I see You testing my growth today."

But here's what I've learned: people's choices don't equal God's rejection. Just because they couldn't handle my worth doesn't mean I don't have it. I'm not just "seen" by God — I'm engraved on His hands. You don't engrave something you plan to forget. That's permanent love.

There's no algorithm, no "perfect woman" checklist, no missed call that can erase that truth. Sometimes rejection hurts not because we lost something, but because it reminded us of every other "no" that came before it. It's the echo that stings.

But God has this way of turning "no" into next. Sometimes rejection is protection. Sometimes it's redirection. And sometimes it's divine intervention, saving you from heartbreaks that looked holy but weren't healthy.

So, when that "not chosen" feeling starts to creep back in, I remind myself:

It's not rejection — it's God's protection.

Every "no" that shut me out was actually Him sheltering me. I've stopped calling it rejection and started calling it release. Because when God removes what's not aligned, it's only to make space for what is.

Meditation:

Think of one moment of rejection that still stings. Picture yourself holding it out to Jesus. Hear Him whisper:

> "Their no doesn't change My yes.
> I have chosen you, always."

Survival Tip – Reframe the No:

1. Write down the rejection that hurt you — name it.

2. Next to it, write one way it might have been protection.

3. Pray: "Lord, teach me to trust the redirection even when the no hurts."

Connection Challenge:

If you feel comfortable, share with a safe friend: "That no hurt, but I'm starting to see it as protection." If not, write it in your journal and ask God to show you how He's using it for your good.

▌ Song of the Day – "Ex-Factor" by Lauryn Hill

For when rejection stirs up questions — but also as a reminder that you're not the only one who's felt it, and you can come out stronger. Let the honesty in her voice remind you: your story doesn't end in heartbreak — it's only getting remixed for healing.

Monica Lynese Guthrie Purchase

DAY 18 – WHEN HEALING FINALLY BEGINS

Scripture:

"He heals the brokenhearted and binds up their wounds."
– Psalm 147:3

Reflection:

Healing doesn't happen in one big swoop—it's slow, layered, and sometimes downright messy. It's not "poof, I'm fine now." Nope. For me, it looked more like taking two steps forward, one step back, crying in therapy on Tuesday, and cracking jokes about it by Friday.

I used to think healing meant never being triggered again. But real healing for me looked like little choices: showing up to therapy when I wanted to isolate, telling my story instead of swallowing it, giving myself permission to cry and then—permission to laugh again. Some days I was full of faith, other days I was just full of tears and caffeine. But I showed up anyway.

And here's what I've realized—even this devotional, this vulnerability, is part of my healing. The enemy would love for me to keep quiet, to hold it in, to pretend I've got it all together. But the more I share my stories, the more I see how God is using my pain to help somebody else heal too. What the devil tried to use to isolate me, God is using to illuminate His glory through me.

There came a moment when I realized something had shifted. I wasn't replaying the old rejection reel in my head anymore. The sting didn't vanish, but it softened. My prayers changed too—from "Why not me?" to "Lord, keep me ready for what You have." That's when I knew healing had begun.

Healing doesn't mean forgetting—it means remembering without reliving. It's when you can look back at what almost broke you and see how God used it to build you. Healing is when you can tell your story and not cry the whole way through (maybe tear up a little, but not ugly cry).

And listen... the same God who allowed the breaking is the same God who specializes in restoration. He didn't just put the pieces back together—He made something stronger, wiser, and more whole. So if you're still in the middle of it, don't rush the process. Healing doesn't come in a day—it comes in layers. But layer by layer, you're becoming the healed version of yourself you prayed for.

Meditation:

Picture the wound you've carried like a scar. Now imagine Jesus placing His hand over it—not erasing it, but sealing it with love. Whisper:

"Lord, thank You for binding up my wounds.
Teach me to see healing as a process, not perfection."

Survival Tip – Walk in Healing:

1. Name one step you've already taken toward healing (therapy, prayer, boundaries, self-care).

2. Write down one next step you can commit to.

3. Celebrate progress, not perfection.*

Connection Challenge:

If you feel comfortable, share your healing milestone with a safe person:

"I used to be stuck in this, but now I'm moving forward."

If not, write it in your journal as a testimony between you and God.

▌Song of the Day – "Healed" by Donald Lawrence & The Tri-City Singers

A declaration that your story doesn't end in pain—it ends in purpose. Let this song remind you: every scar tells the story of a battle you survived. You didn't just make it through—you healed through.

DAY 19 – WHEN CHRISTMAS FEELS QUIET

Scripture:

"*Be still, and know that I am God.*"
– Psalm 46:10

Reflection:

There's something about Christmas morning that can feel both holy and heavy. The world seems to pause—carols are playing, cinnamon rolls are baking, and everyone's posting family photos in matching pajamas. Meanwhile, your house might be... quiet. Peaceful, yes—but also a little too still.

I've had those Christmas mornings. No little feet running through the house. No partner reaching for me with a sleepy "Merry Christmas, babe." Just me, my coffee, and my thoughts. And while I thanked God for breath and life, I'd be lying if I said there wasn't a sting tucked in the gratitude.

Some years, I filled the silence with sound—music, movies, or FaceTiming my family. Other years, I sat in the quiet and let the tears fall because pretending didn't make it better. Loneliness doesn't disappear just because it's December 25th—it just dresses up in tinsel and sparkles for the day.

But one year, something shifted. I realized the quiet wasn't punishment—it was invitation. An invitation to see God in a new way. To sit with Him without the noise, without the rush, without the comparison. The same God who met the shepherds in the stillness of the night meets us in the stillness of our rooms.

Now, I may light a candle, journal a little, or just laugh at the fact that the best part of being single on Christmas is that I can sleep in—no one's waking me up at 6 a.m. to open presents! I'm learning to find the small pleasures in my singleness, even when there's no one to exchange gifts with. Because the truth is, I'm finally learning to love the gift of me—and all God created me to be.

And you know what else? I'm learning to break the cycles—the ones that say I have to spend every Christmas feeling less than, forgotten, or left out. The ones that make me scroll and compare my behind-the-scenes to someone else's highlight reel. God is teaching me that peace is my portion and joy is my inheritance. The silence that once reminded me of lack now reminds me of His presence.

The quiet still comes, but now it feels less like loneliness and more like peace. It's where I remember that even in the stillness, God is here—and that's enough.

Meditation:

Close your eyes and picture your space this Christmas. Hear the silence as an invitation, not a punishment. Whisper this prayer:

> "Lord, meet me in the quiet. Help me see You in the stillness and remind me that this silence is sacred, not sad."

Survival Tip – Find Beauty in the Quiet:

1. Play soft music that lifts your spirit—no sad songs! (You know which ones I mean ▮).

2. Write down three things you're grateful for today, not someday.

3. Step outside, breathe the crisp air, and whisper, "I'm still here, and God is still good."

Connection Challenge:

If you can, call or text someone else who might be alone today—remind them they're seen and loved. If you're not up for talking, write a note of gratitude to God for getting you through another year of growing stronger.

▌ Song of the Day: "Cycles" – Jonathan McReynolds

This Christmas, break the cycle of sadness and comparison. Let this song be your anthem of renewal—because God specializes in doing something new, even on the same old days.

Monica Lynese Guthrie Purchase

DAY 20 – WHEN GOALS GO UNMET

Scripture:

"*Though it linger, wait for it; it will certainly come and will not delay.*"
– Habakkuk 2:3

Reflection:

Whew, chile... the end of the year will have you in your feelings if you let it. The vision board is still hanging up, and half the stuff on it didn't even make it off the sticky note. The job I thought I'd have by summer—nope. The book I swore I'd finish—still sitting in my drafts. The relationship I just knew was "it"? Yeah... that one turned into a testimony and a therapy bill.

Every December, I'd catch myself saying, "Next year will be different." Then January came, and it looked a whole lot like the December I just left. That cycle will have you thinking you failed—but let me tell you what God had to tell me: unmet doesn't mean denied.

Some prayers are marinating. Some goals are aging like fine wine. And some? They were never mine to begin with. God's timing has never been about my calendar—it's about my character. He's developing the strength and wisdom I'll need to handle what I'm asking for.

It's like a good pot of chili. The first day it's fine, but let it sit overnight, and baby, the flavor deepens. That's what God is doing with my prayers—letting them soak, simmer, and season. The waiting isn't punishment; it's preparation.

And if I'm honest, there were days I told the Lord, "Now listen, I don't want to be Your strongest soldier no more! I'll gladly take the easy assignment for once!" But even in those moments, I knew He wasn't withholding—He was working.

So now I'm learning to thank Him for what didn't happen yet. Because the "not yet" might just be His way of protecting me from something that wasn't ready—or from me not being ready. Cycles break when I stop beating myself up for what didn't happen and start asking, "Lord, what are You building in me while I wait?"

Meditation:

Think of one goal—or relationship—you carried into this year that's still undone. Hold it before God and whisper:

> "Lord, if this is still for me, breathe life into it. If it's not, give me peace to release it. Break every cycle that keeps me stuck in disappointment."

Survival Tip – Reset the Narrative:

1. Write down three wins from this year—big or small.

2. Circle one goal (or desire) you'll carry forward, and cross out one you're releasing.

3. Say it out loud: "I am not stuck. God is still writing my story."

Connection Challenge:

If you feel comfortable, share one of your wins with a friend—it doesn't have to be huge. If not, write it down as a private celebration between you and God.

▌ Song of the Day: "Moving Forward" – Israel Houghton

A soulful reminder that even if some goals didn't come to pass, you're not standing still—you're stepping into what's next. Because every move forward, no matter how small, breaks another cycle.

DAY 21 – WHEN THE NEW YEAR FEELS HEAVY BEFORE IT BEGINS

Scripture:

"See, I am doing a new thing! Now it springs up; do you not perceive it? I am making a way in the wilderness and streams in the wasteland."
– Isaiah 43:19

Reflection:

January 1st doesn't erase December 31st. The bills, the heartbreak, the loneliness—they don't vanish just because the ball dropped and the calendar flipped. Just because the countdown ended doesn't mean we've suddenly been transported to a land of confetti and sunshine.

It's not The Wizard of Oz, where Dorothy opens the door and the world bursts into Technicolor. It's not even The Wiz, where you can click your heels and end up home safe. Honestly, some years feel more like Wicked—where the story isn't simple, the timing isn't perfect, and the lessons come wrapped in chaos.

And me? I'm out here just trying to defy gravity—to rise above the weight of old disappointments, to break out of the same cycles, to believe that something better really can come next.

The truth is, we don't wake up in a brand-new world on January 1st. Most of the time, it's the same life, the same circumstances, the same version of us—just stepping into another year. And that realization can feel heavy.

But here's what God keeps teaching me: a new year isn't magic, but it is a reminder. His mercies are new every morning, not just every January. The beauty isn't in the ball drop—it's in His promise to do a new thing right in the middle of our same old wilderness.

Sometimes that "new thing" doesn't look like open doors or answered prayers. Sometimes it's a quiet shift—a deeper peace, a softer heart, a slower reaction, or a stronger faith. It's the change you don't always notice until you look back and realize, "Wait... I didn't handle that like I used to."

The calendar doesn't hold the power—He does. And when He says He's making a way, He means it. Even when you can't see the path yet, He's already laying the stones under your feet.

Meditation:

Take a deep breath. Picture yourself carrying the baggage of last year. Now imagine laying it at God's feet and walking forward lighter. Whisper:

> "Lord, I release the weight of yesterday. Help me see the new thing You're already doing—even if I don't see the full picture yet."

Survival Tip – Step Small, Step Forward:

1. Write one small, life-giving step you can take this week—rest, therapy, prayer, or a walk.

2. Circle it, and commit to just that one.

3. Declare: "I don't need magic; I need mercy. And His mercy is already here."

Connection Challenge:

If you feel comfortable, tell a trusted friend or mentor one thing you're hoping for in this new year. If not, write it in your journal as a prayer between you and God.

▌Song of the Day: "Golden" – Jill Scott

Because stepping into a new year isn't about perfection—it's about freedom. Living your life like it's golden means showing up intentionally, gracefully, and gratefully... even if the healing is still in progress.

Monica Lynese Guthrie Purchase

DAY 22 – WHEN CHRISTMAS MORNING ISN'T MERRY

Scripture:

"*Rejoice with those who rejoice; mourn with those who mourn. Live in harmony with one another. Do not be proud, but be willing to associate with people of low position. Do not be conceited.*"
– Romans 12:15–16

Reflection:

Christmas morning doesn't always start with excitement — sometimes it starts with your phone buzzing from the family group text. "Merry Christmas!" And you're half-asleep thinking, Why do we do this, y'all? ▊ Then you hop on Facebook or Instagram and see all the happy families in matching pajamas, the couples exchanging gifts, and the kids tearing into presents. It's the annual scroll of wonderment — everyone's highlight reel on full display — and meanwhile, you're just trying to decide if you even feel like getting out of bed.

I've been there. Sitting with my coffee in hand, still in pajamas, watching the morning unfold online while my own house stayed quiet. My kids are grown, my granddaughter's miles away, and my senagers (my parents) are doing their own thing. I love them dearly, but sometimes that quiet hits different. Gratitude and heaviness can coexist in the same heart — and that's okay.

There were mornings I wrestled with guilt. "Why can't I just be content?" Condemnation would whisper that I was being ungrateful — that I should just be happy I have family at all. And while I am thankful, it doesn't erase the ache for what I imagined life would look like by now.

Some years I light a candle, journal a little, and laugh because, hey — at least this means I can sleep in and don't have to assemble a single toy! ▌ I'm learning to find the small pleasures in my singleness, to unwrap the gift of me, and to thank God that even if I don't have someone to exchange gifts with, I still have His presence — and that's the best gift of all.

And when the quiet feels a little too quiet, I think about my mom's favorite movie, The Sound of Music. There's this moment when Julie Andrews sings, "When the dog bites, when the bee stings, when I'm feeling sad..." and she shifts her focus to a few of her favorite things. My mom would light up every time that song came on — and now, I get it. When the day feels heavy, that song reminds me to pause and name a few of my own favorite things: God's faithfulness, my family's laughter, my peace, my purpose, and the fact that I'm still here — still standing, still growing, still loved.

Because Christmas may not always be merry, but it can still be meaningful — and sometimes, finding joy starts with remembering the things (and people) you already have.

Meditation:

Take a deep breath and look around you — what's here, right now, that reflects God's presence? Whisper:

"Lord, thank You for being with me in every season. Teach me to find peace in Your presence, even when my circumstances feel quiet."

Survival Tip – Presence Over Perfection:

1. Light a candle (or not — light the metaphorical one in your heart) and pray for those you love — near or far.

2. Write a list of three blessings you can see in your current season.

3. When comparison creeps in, give yourself permission to laugh, to cry, and then remind yourself: "Even this quiet morning holds purpose."

Connection Challenge:

Text or call someone you love — a friend, a family member, or someone who might also be alone today — and remind them they're seen and loved. If a call feels like too much, send a quick voice note or a simple heart emoji. Small kindnesses ripple.

▮ Song of the Day: "My Favorite Things" – Luther Vandross

Because when the morning feels quiet, gratitude can still make music. Sometimes joy begins by counting your favorite things — and realizing God was one of them all along.

DAY 23 – WHEN THE AFTER-CHRISTMAS LETDOWN HITS

Scripture:

"Nehemiah said, 'Go and enjoy choice food and sweet drinks, and send some to those who have nothing prepared. This day is holy to our Lord. Do not grieve, for the joy of the Lord is your strength.'"
– Nehemiah 8:10

Reflection:

There's a strange quiet after Christmas. The wrapping paper is gone, the leftovers are in the fridge, and the hype disappears overnight. I've felt that letdown hit hard. One year, I remember sitting in my room the day after Christmas, scrolling through Facebook while everyone else's feeds still seemed full of family joy. Mine felt quiet, and I felt flat. My phone was dryer than the Sahara Desert—no calls, no texts, no invites. Just me, my thoughts, and the silence.

The holiday "high" fades fast. One minute it's laughter and lights, and the next it's just... stillness. As a single woman, that's often when loneliness creeps in hardest—when the noise dies down and the quiet reminds you of what's missing.

And I'll be honest—sometimes I'll catch a commercial or movie scene of a perfect family Christmas and feel that twinge. You know, the "why not me?" moment. But that's when I breathe and remind myself that joy isn't found in what's happening around me—it's in Who's holding me through it.

Nehemiah didn't tell the people to stop grieving because everything was perfect. He said, "The joy of the Lord is your strength," in spite of what wasn't. Joy is a decision, not a download. It doesn't always fall into your lap—you have to reach for it. Some days that choice looks like worship when you'd rather wallow. Other days it's laughing at a silly video, watching your favorite movie, or letting yourself smile even when tears were there first.

Joy doesn't deny reality—it just changes how you walk through it. The wrapping paper may be gone, but the promise of joy still stands.

Meditation:

Close your eyes. Picture your quiet space—the tree dimmed, the dishes done, the world settling. Whisper:

> "Lord, when the celebration fades, remind me that You remain. Let Your joy be the strength that carries me into what's next."

Survival Tip – Choose Joy on Purpose:

1. Do one simple thing that makes you smile—blast a song, sip a latte, or take a walk.

2. Write down three small moments from Christmas that made you grateful.

3. When sadness knocks, reread that list and remember: His joy still belongs to you.

Connection Challenge:

Reach out to one person you haven't talked to in a while—share something funny, sweet, or honest about your week. Connection keeps the joy alive.

❚ Song of the Day: "Joy" – Whitney Houston & The Georgia Mass Choir

Because joy isn't seasonal—it's the steady strength that carries you long after the holiday lights fade.

Monica Lynese Guthrie Purchase

DAY 24 – WHEN YOUR BIRTHDAY FEELS BITTERSWEET

Scripture:

" I praise you because I am fearfully and wonderfully made; your works are wonderful, I know that full well."
– Psalm 139:14

Reflection:

Having a birthday on New Year's Eve is a blessing and a burden. The whole world celebrates—but it's not always celebrating you. And as the years pass, it can feel bittersweet. Another birthday without the husband I hoped for. Another year where the biggest gift still comes from my mama. Another December 31st where I thought life would look different by now.

I've shed tears on my birthday—not because I'm ungrateful for life, but because the ache of what's missing felt louder than the noise of what's present. And if I'm really honest, one of my deepest fears has been leaving this earth without making an impact.

What if I live all these years, go through all this life, and nobody's world is better because I was here?

That fear has followed me into more than one birthday. It crept in when I saw others "further along" in life, posting their wins, their families, their accomplishments. It whispered that maybe I hadn't done enough. Maybe I hadn't been enough.

But the truth I keep circling back to is this: my very existence is proof of impact. The fact that I'm still here means there's still work God has for me to do. My children, my grandchild, the students I've poured into, the friends who've leaned on me, the strangers I've encouraged—all of them carry pieces of my life with them. And that is impact.

Every birthday is not just another year passed—it's another year of purpose preserved. God decided the world still needed my presence. And that alone is worth celebrating.

Meditation:

Picture God smiling over you on the day you were born, whispering: "I created you on purpose, for purpose." Whisper back: "Lord, thank You for the gift of life. Help me see the impact I've already made, and the purpose still ahead."

Survival Tip – Celebrate the Impact You've Made:

1. Write down 3 ways your life has already left a mark (family, work, ministry, friendships).

2. Write down 1 way you want to leave impact in the year ahead.

3. Remember: impact isn't measured in fame or numbers—it's measured in lives touched.

Connection Challenge:

If you feel comfortable, share with a friend or family member: "You're part of the reason I know my life has made a difference."

▌ Song of the Day: "I Was Here" – Beyoncé.

Because birthdays are not just about getting older— they're about remembering that your presence matters, your story matters, and your impact is already being written.

Monica Lynese Guthrie Purchase

DAY 25 – WHEN THE YEAR FINALLY TURNS

Scripture:

"*Because of the Lord's great love we are not consumed, for his compassions never fail. They are new every morning; great is your faithfulness.*"
– Lamentations 3:22–23

Reflection:

The clock strikes midnight, fireworks light up the sky, and "Auld Lang Syne" starts playing. Couples are kissing, people are hugging, everybody's crying and shouting "Happy New Year!"—and I'm sitting there like, "WHO CARES!? So what—I'm alone... again this year."

That's real. The hype of the moment can make the ache louder. I've had years where I looked around and felt that familiar sting—watching everyone else coupled up while I carried the same unmet prayers into another January. Another cycle of "next year will be different," only to feel the same ache at the stroke of midnight.

But here's what God keeps teaching me: my worth is not defined by who kisses me when the ball drops, or whether the countdown looks picture-perfect. The new year doesn't magically change my circumstances, but His mercy is new every morning. That's a promise that doesn't depend on fireworks, champagne, or confetti.

I've also had to learn that joy is a choice. Just like after Christmas, I can choose despair or I can choose hope. Some years, that choice was made through tears. Other years, it was through shaky faith and whispered prayers. But each time, choosing joy meant I wasn't letting the cycle win.

Stepping into a new year isn't about erasing the old one—it's about walking in fresh mercy. The world is celebrating time changing, but as believers, we celebrate that God never changes. And He has promised to do a new thing, not just every January, but every single morning.

Meditation:

Take a deep breath as the year begins. Whisper: "Lord, I release the weight of last year. I choose joy. Thank You that Your mercies are new every morning—carry me into this year with fresh hope."

Survival Tip – Begin with Mercy:

1. Write down one area of your life where you desperately need new mercy this year.

2. Pray over it specifically.

3. Declare: "I don't need everything fixed—I need His mercy. And His mercy is already here."

Connection Challenge:

If you feel comfortable, share your mercy prayer with a trusted friend who can agree with you. If not, write it in your journal and revisit it throughout the year.

▌ Song of the Day: "Optimistic" – Sounds of Blackness.

Because while the world is singing "Auld Lang Syne," you can raise a different anthem—hope, joy, and faith in a God who makes all things new.

Monica Lynese Guthrie Purchase

DAY 26 | WHEN THE DAY FEELS BOTH HOLY AND HEAVY

Scripture:

" The Lord is close to the brokenhearted and saves those who are crushed in spirit."
— Psalm 34:18 (NIV)

Reflection

Some days hold both sunlight and shadows. You wake up grateful, but your heart still tugs with the weight of what isn't. The Christmas glow is fading, New Year's is whispering your name, and in between sits this sacred ache — that space where joy and longing bump shoulders. A day that feels both holy and heavy.

I remember feeling that way one holiday in Jamaica. The sun was shining, laughter was spilling across the beach, and my chosen family surrounded me with love. It was my first birthday trip, and for once, I actually let people celebrate me without apology. No hiding behind busyness. No brushing off the compliments. I leaned in. And it was beautiful.

But even in that joy, there was a small ache — a reminder of prayers still waiting for answers, of people who couldn't be there, of the quiet wish for the kind of love I'd watched others unwrap year after year. And listen... the men were fine, but not checkin' for me! ▌ I had to laugh to keep from crying, because sometimes that's just how life be.

Still, somewhere between the waves and the worship, I felt Him. God wasn't asking me to choose between joy and ache — He was sitting right there with me in both. The tears didn't mean I lacked faith; they meant my heart was still open. My tears were worship. My honesty was praise.

There's something holy about holding both — the gratitude for what is and the grief for what isn't — and still saying, "God, I trust You right here." Sometimes that's the most sacred offering we can give

Meditation

Your heaviness doesn't cancel holiness.

Both can live here.

Let God meet you in the middle — between what you hoped for and what still hurts.

Survival Tip – Hold Space for Both

If the day feels like a tug-of-war between gratitude and grief, pause and breathe. Speak this aloud:

> "Both can live here."
> Then write one sentence of thanks for what is, and one prayer for what's still becoming.

Connection Challenge

Reach out to someone who's had a hard season and simply ask, "How are you really?" Don't rush to fix or preach — sometimes the ministry is just being there.

▌Song of the Day "Better Days" – Le'Andria Johnson

Because even when your heart feels heavy, hope hums beneath the surface. This song reminds you that the ache won't last forever — God is still writing beauty into your story, even here, even now.

Monica Lynese Guthrie Purchase

DAY 27 | WHEN THE WEIGHT HITS

Scripture:

"Come to Me, all you who are weary and burdened, and I will give you rest."
— Matthew 11:28 (NIV)

Reflection

You ever notice how the emotional crash sometimes comes after the celebration? The decorations are still up, the leftovers are still in the fridge, but the joy feels like it clocked out early. One day everything is full of laughter, food, and family — and then suddenly it's quiet. The phone stops buzzing. The people go home. The noise settles. And the weight hits.

It's not always sadness — sometimes it's exhaustion, disappointment, or the realization that another year has passed and the thing you prayed for still hasn't come. I've had days like that where I tried to "push through" and pretend everything was fine, only to end up crying on the couch with cold coffee and a full heart that just needed release.

That's when I learned that crashing doesn't mean you've failed. It just means you're human. Even joy can be heavy when you've been carrying hope for a long time. I used to feel guilty for feeling down after something good, as if gratitude and grief couldn't coexist. But they can. God is not offended by our fatigue — He invites us to bring it to Him.

And while you're doing that, give yourself grace. You don't have to bounce back overnight. You don't have to smile through everything. Rest is not weakness; it's stewardship of your soul. I haven't always done that well — I've been my own harshest critic when what I really needed was compassion. But grace allows room for healing. So today, be gentle with yourself.

Sometimes rest isn't about sleeping more; it's about exhaling — about laying down the mental load of trying to hold everything together. Jesus never said, "Fake it till you make it." He said, "Come to Me." So when the weight hits, don't run from it. Bring it to the One who can actually carry it.

Meditation

Your crash isn't the end of your strength — it's the invitation to God's.

Survival Tip – Rest Without Guilt

When your energy dips and your emotions feel heavy, don't power through. Stop. Breathe. Turn on calm music or step outside for five minutes. Say this prayer out loud:

> "Lord, I'm tired. But You're not. Be strength where I'm weak today — and help me show myself the same grace You've shown me."

Connection Challenge

Share a real moment with someone you trust — not the polished version, but the honest one. You never know who might say, "Me too."

❚ Song of the Day "Wanna Be Happy?" – Kirk Franklin

A reminder that healing often starts with honesty. Sometimes joy begins the moment you stop pretending and let God meet you where you really are.

Monica Lynese Guthrie Purchase

DAY 28 | WHEN HOPE STILL FLICKERS

Scripture:

"A bruised reed He will not break, and a smoldering wick He will not snuff out."
— Isaiah 42:3 (NIV)

Reflection

Hope doesn't always roar. Sometimes it whispers. Sometimes it's that tiny spark still glowing under the ashes when life has burned hot and hard.

I've had seasons where I was convinced the fire had gone out — when prayers felt repetitive and faith felt heavy. I would say, "Lord, I know You're good, but right now I'm tired of saying it." There have been nights when I wanted to tap the mic like, "Hello, Lord? Is this thing on? Do You hear me? Do You see me? You remember I'm still down here single, right — while some people are on their third and fourth marriage?"

I laugh about it now, but in those moments, the ache was real. That kind of honesty doesn't scare God, though. He can handle every sigh, every question, every "Why not me yet?" Because even in those raw, unfiltered moments, He's still tending the flame.

There were years I thought the light had gone completely dark in me. I was showing up for everyone else — family, ministry, work — but inside, I was running on fumes. Then one day, God sent the smallest reminder: a verse I'd forgotten, a song on the radio, a text from a friend that said, "Just thinking about you." And it hit me — that was Him, fanning the flame.

Maybe you've been there too — where you don't have a full shout left, just a whisper of "Lord, help me hold on." I've learned that's enough. Because the same God who spoke galaxies into existence is gentle enough to cup your tiny flame and say, "I'm not letting this go out."

So even when hope only flickers, don't despise it. That faint light still carries power.

Meditation

A flicker of hope in God's hands can light an entire future.

Survival Tip – Fan the Flame

Write down one thing — no matter how small — that gives you hope right now. It might be a person, a promise, or even a memory. Place it somewhere visible and whisper,

> "It's not over."
> Let that reminder fan your flame when life feels dim.

Connection Challenge

Send a message to someone who's been your "spark" this year. Tell them, "You helped keep my light on." Gratitude not only honors them — it strengthens your own hope too.

▌**Song of the Day** "Encourage Yourself" – Donald Lawrence & The Tri-City Singers

A reminder that even when no one else can see your flame, you can still speak life to it. Sometimes the best encouragement comes from the voice inside you — partnered with the God who refuses to let your fire die.

DAY 29 | WHEN THE STRETCH FEELS ENDLESS

Scripture:

"Let perseverance finish its work so that you may be mature and complete, not lacking anything."
— James 1:4 (NIV)

Reflection

There are seasons when it feels like God's favorite workout for me is stretching.

Not the peaceful yoga kind, either — the kind that makes you say, "Lord, if You pull me one more inch, I might pop."

Sometimes the waiting feels like an Olympic event — faith, flexibility, and endurance all being tested at once. I've had stretches that lasted months, others that felt like years. Seasons where I thought, surely this is the breakthrough, only to realize it was just another rep in God's gym of growth.

And whew — let me be honest — there have been several times I've told the Lord, "Okay, I'm strong enough! I don't want to be Your strongest soldier anymore. I'm good with being a regular, average Christian with a few blessings and no trials!"

But even in that frustration, God keeps reminding me — He's not trying to make me suffer; He's strengthening what's sacred inside me.

I've prayed, fasted, journaled, and worshiped, but still felt like I was treading water between "promise" and "manifestation." Yet somehow, even in the ache, something holy happens: I start seeing that the stretch is proof I'm not stuck. God only stretches what He intends to strengthen.

It's in those moments I hear Him whisper, "I'm not punishing you; I'm preparing you." Growth doesn't always feel like glory — it feels like resistance. And sometimes that resistance is the very thing developing the endurance for the blessing you've been asking for.

So when you're tempted to snap under pressure, remember — He's not stretching you to break you; He's stretching you to bless you.

Meditation

The same God who called you to it is stretching you through it.

Survival Tip – Trust the Stretch

When the waiting feels unbearable, pause and write down one thing you've gained during this stretch — patience, perspective, peace. You may not see the full picture yet, but that growth is evidence that God's work isn't wasted.

Connection Challenge

Call or text someone who's in their own waiting season and remind them, "You're not breaking — you're being built." Sometimes the best encouragement is letting someone know they're not the only one feeling the pull.

❚ Song of the Day "Keep the Faith" – Faith Evans

Smooth and soulful, it's a reminder to stay grounded and trust that every stretch has purpose. Keep holding on — because what's stretching you today is strengthening you for tomorrow.

Monica Lynese Guthrie Purchase

DAY 30 | WHEN YOU REFLECT ON THE YEAR THAT'S PASSED

Scripture:

"Forget the former things; do not dwell on the past. See, I am doing a new thing! Now it springs up; do you not perceive it?"
— Isaiah 43:18–19 (NIV)

Reflection

Every December 31st, the world gathers to count down seconds — but I've learned that the real countdown starts inside the heart. There's something sacred about pausing between what was and what's about to be.

For me, December 31st isn't just the end of the year — it's also my birthday. Another year older. Another year of lessons, love, and learning. And if I'm being honest, for a long time it was also another reminder that I was still single. I went from saying I'd be remarried by 40, to maybe by 45... and now here I am at 51 — still waiting, still believing, and still learning to find joy in the in-between.

There were years when that realization hit hard. When I watched others post engagement announcements, wedding pictures, and "his and hers" matching pajama sets, while I was just praying my Amazon cart would count as company. ▌ It wasn't bitterness — it was that quiet ache of "Lord, what about me?" But even in those moments, God gently reminded me: "My best days aren't behind me — they're just ahead."

Reflection used to make me anxious; it felt like a highlight reel of everything that didn't happen — the job I didn't get, the relationship I didn't have, the plans that didn't pan out. But over time, I realized reflection isn't about reliving pain — it's about recognizing progress. It's looking back not to stay there, but to thank God that you're not who you were when the year began.

So this year, give yourself grace for what didn't go perfectly. You survived things that tried to break you. You healed in places you once hid. You learned to set boundaries, forgive differently, and love yourself deeper. That's growth worth celebrating.

Before the ball drops, sit still for a moment. Take a deep breath. Whisper, "Thank You, Lord, for keeping me — through it all." Then exhale the pressure to have it all figured out. God's not done writing your story; He's just turning the page.

Meditation

Reflection isn't about regret — it's about recognition.

See what God has done, and trust what He's still doing.

Survival Tip – Reflect with Grace

Write a thank-you list instead of a resolution list.

Thank God for every lesson, every person, every open door — and even the ones He closed. Gratitude shifts your focus from what's missing to what's meaningful.

Connection Challenge

Reach out to someone who's been part of your journey this year. Tell them, "I see how God used you to bless me."

You'll both step into the new year lighter.

❚ **Song of the Day** "Better" – Jessica Reedy

A soft, soulful anthem reminding you that no matter what didn't happen, you're stronger, wiser, and better because of it. Because the truth is — God didn't just carry you through this year... He prepared you for what's next.

DAY 31 | WHEN THE CLOCK STRIKES MIDNIGHT

Scripture:

"About midnight Paul and Silas were praying and singing hymns to God, and the other prisoners were listening to them. Suddenly there was a violent earthquake... and everyone's chains came loose."
— Acts 16:25–26 (NIV)

Reflection

There's something about midnight. The world counts it as the end of one year and the beginning of another — but in the spirit, midnight has always been the hour of movement.

Breakthroughs happen at midnight. Deliverance happens at midnight. God shifts things when the clock strikes twelve.

For years, I've spent New Year's Eve in church — praising, praying, and shouting my way into another year. Some years surrounded by family and friends, and others, quietly alone. And when the countdown hits, there's that familiar rush — voices shouting

"Happy New Year!" hugs, couples kissing, spouses embracing first.

And me? I've learned to just wait my turn.

I used to laugh and say I felt like Cinderella — standing in my heels, dress still sparkling, but no carriage waiting outside. Midnight came, and instead of a prince, it was just me... and Jesus. Year after year after year.

But honestly? He's been the most faithful one yet.

There were nights I felt the sting of loneliness right there in the sanctuary, watching everyone else pair off while I just clapped and smiled. But there were also nights when the Spirit wrapped me up so tight, it felt like a holy hug. I realized midnight wasn't just the world's moment — it was my meeting place with God.

Because at midnight, chains break. At midnight, the Bridegroom comes. At midnight, God moves on behalf of His people. And at midnight, even if no one reaches for my hand, Heaven does.

So now, when the clock strikes twelve, I lift my hands instead of lowering my head. I whisper, "Thank You,

Lord, for another year to become who You called me to be."

Midnight isn't just another countdown — it's a holy reminder that I'm still chosen, still loved, and still becoming.

Meditation

Midnight is when heaven moves.

When the noise quiets, God speaks.

Survival Tip – Worship Before You Wish

When the clock strikes twelve, pause before you shout or text. Whisper your gratitude to God first — thank Him for every chain that's already breaking and every blessing that's on the way.

Connection Challenge

Find one person who's starting the new year feeling unseen or forgotten and send them a midnight message of hope:

> "God hasn't forgotten you. You're on His timeline."

❙ Song of the Day "You Waited" – Travis Greene

A heartfelt worship moment that echoes the power of midnight — when God's patience meets your surrender and His love shows up right on time.

Monica Lynese Guthrie Purchase

DAY 32 | WHEN YOU START AGAIN

Scripture:

"*Because of the Lord's great love we are not consumed, for His compassions never fail. They are new every morning; great is Your faithfulness.*"
— Lamentations 3:22–23 (NIV)

Reflection

The confetti's been swept away. The candles are out. The glitter from last night's praise or party is still on your sleeve. It's quiet now — just you, a new calendar page, and the sound of your own heartbeat reminding you: You made it.

Starting again doesn't always come with fanfare. Sometimes it's just breathing a little deeper and saying, "Okay, Lord, what's next?" After the high of midnight fades, this is where real beginnings are born.

Every year, people rush to make resolutions — lose weight, save money, find love, be better. And while there's nothing wrong with wanting more, I've learned that what matters most isn't the list you make on January 1st — it's the heart you carry into every day after. God's not impressed by our performance; He's drawn to our posture.

There have been mornings when I woke up after all the celebration and felt the weight of unanswered prayers. Still single. Still waiting. Still believing. And for a long time, that still came with a question: "Still, Lord? Still? When is it my turn?"

But lately, God's been shifting that still in me. It's no longer a question — it's a position. I've moved from "Still, God?" to "I'll stay still, God." No more rushing into relationships, situationships, or temporary fixes just to feel seen. No more chasing moments that don't align with His mission. If He says wait, I'll wait. If He says rest, I'll rest. Still doesn't mean stuck — it means surrendered.

There's a peace that comes when you stop forcing what's not flowing. And that's where the anointing falls — right in the middle of your stillness. The place where tears dry, burdens lift, and His presence wraps you up like a warm embrace. It's that "just You and me, Lord" space your spirit's been craving.

So this year, I don't just want a new start. I want a fresh pour. I want His oil to touch every dry and waiting place in my life. Because with His anointing, even stillness becomes sacred movement.

Meditation

Stillness isn't the absence of movement —

it's the awareness of God's hand in every detail.

Survival Tip – Wait for the Pour

Before you make a single resolution, make room.

Ask God to anoint your next steps, and don't move until you sense His peace pushing you forward.

Connection Challenge

Invite a friend to join you in a "Stillness Check-In."

Spend 10 minutes in silence, journaling what God whispers when you stop striving.

❙ Song of the Day "Still" – Jonathan McReynolds

A heartfelt reminder that even when life feels uncertain and overwhelming, God's presence hasn't moved. The lyrics invite you to rest in His calm:

"You're not a God of confusion, You're not a God of fear... so even when I'm restless, I'm gonna be still."

DAY 33 | WHEN FAITH FEELS FRAGILE

Scripture:

"*I do believe; help me overcome my unbelief!*"
— Mark 9:24 (NIV)

Reflection

The new-year glow fades fast. The gym isn't as full. The vision board that once looked like a bold declaration now feels more like a dream. The "this is my year!" pep talk starts to run headfirst into real life — bills, busyness, a few unexpected detours, and all those incidentals and oopsadentals (you know, the stuff we really didn't plan for).

Faith feels easy when everything's flowing. But when the waiting drags, the prayers seem unanswered, and life doesn't match your expectation, that faith can start to wobble. I've been there — staring at my journal or worship playlist, trying to stir something up that just feels... quiet.

And sometimes, when life is really lifin', I find myself wanting to call Heaven's Hotline just to make sure they got my last prayer request — like, "Hello? Just checking if y'all received that one I sent about three weeks ago?" ⏸

There have been seasons when I thought my faith was broken because I didn't feel strong. But over time, I've learned something: fragile faith is still faith. The woman in Mark 5 only touched the hem of His garment. Peter started to sink but still reached for Jesus' hand. The father in Mark 9 said, "I believe — help my unbelief." And Jesus still moved.

And the Word reminds us — faith doesn't have to be massive to matter. Jesus said if we have faith the size of a grain of mustard seed, we can speak to mountains and they'll move. Not even the whole seed — just the grain. Sometimes, all I've had left in me was that one little grain, but even that small faith holds weight in the eyes of the Lord.

Because what seems tiny to us still carries power when it's anchored in Him. That means God doesn't need my faith to be flawless; He just wants it to be honest.

Some days, my prayers sound like declarations. Other days, they sound like, "Lord, I'm trying... I'm doing the best I can with what I got." And you know what? He honors both.

There have been days I've whispered, "God, I know You can, but will You?" and others when I've said, "I don't see You, but I still choose You." It's in those fragile moments that I've seen His strength most clearly — when I stopped pretending and simply let Him hold me.

If your faith feels fragile right now, you're not failing — you're human. And God's not waiting for you to pull yourself together; He's already in the cracks, holding the pieces.

Meditation

Even fragile faith can move mountains —

because it's not the size of your faith,

it's the size of your God.

Survival Tip – Hold the Grain

Be honest in your prayers. Don't perform faith — practice it.

Tell God exactly where it hurts, where you're tired,

and where you need Him to help your unbelief.

Connection Challenge

Find a faith partner — someone who can remind you of God's promises when your faith starts to flicker.

Sometimes you just need a borrowed belief until yours grows strong again.

Song of the Day "Help Me" – Tamela Mann

A soul-stirring cry of surrender that captures this very moment — that space between belief and breakthrough. It's the kind of song you play when your heart says, "Lord, I still trust You, even when I'm trembling."

Monica Lynese Guthrie Purchase

DAY 34 | WHEN PEACE BECOMES A PRIORITY

Scripture:

" You will keep in perfect peace all who trust in You, all whose thoughts are fixed on You."
— Isaiah 26:3 (NLT)

Reflection

The Christmas season has a way of stirring up everything at once — the lights, the laughter, the family gatherings... and if we're honest, a little chaos too. Between the shopping, the schedules, and the social media highlight reels, it's easy to lose focus and forget that peace is the gift we were promised when Jesus — the Prince of Peace — was born.

There comes a point when peace stops being a luxury and starts being a lifeline. When you've cried the tears, prayed the prayers, sent the texts, deleted the texts (and maybe sent one more after that 🙄), and realized — protecting your peace is protecting your purpose.

I've learned that peace isn't found in the absence of problems; it's found in the presence of God. There have been times I let chaos rent space in my head and heart — replaying conversations, questioning decisions, or trying to fix what I didn't break. And all it ever cost me was peace.

There was a season when I said yes to too many people and too many things that left me drained. I'd give out of obligation, show up out of guilt, and call it "ministry" when really, it was me people-pleasing in the name of service. Whew! ⏸♀️☐ But the Holy Spirit had to remind me: peace is not passive — it's protective.

And sometimes, protecting your peace means refusing to have yet another conversation with someone who still won't take accountability. Because peace is letting your "no" be no and your "yes" be yes — without explanation, debate, or guilt. It's no longer climbing onto the emotional roller coaster someone else insists on riding every day. It's learning to wave from the platform, whisper "Not my monkey, not my circus," and keep it moving — with grace and love.

Because grace doesn't mean access. Love doesn't mean losing yourself. Sometimes grace is quiet distance, and love is releasing people to grow on their own. You can honor God, honor others, and still honor the peace He's placed within you.

So while the world is wrapping presents, I'm unwrapping peace — that deep, still calm that only comes from knowing Who's really in control. I don't need perfect plans or picture-perfect moments. I just need Emmanuel — God with me — and that's more than enough.

Peace is not the absence of noise — it's the ability to hear God's whisper in the middle of it.

Meditation

Peace doesn't just happen.

It's something you decide to protect, nurture, and practice every day —

especially in this season when the world tells you to rush and overextend.

Survival Tip – Protect the Gift

Guard your space and your spirit.

Before you say yes to anything, ask,

"Does this protect my peace or cost it?"

If it costs it — reconsider.

Connection Challenge

Reach out to someone who brings calm instead of chaos.

Spend time with people who speak peace and grace into you, not drain it from you.

▌Song of the Day: "Be Still" – Yolanda Adams

A soothing reminder that real peace isn't the absence of problems — it's the presence of God. In her signature warm, soulful tone, Yolanda invites you to quiet your spirit and rest in the assurance that God is still in control. When the noise of life gets loud and your heart starts racing, let this song minister to you. Breathe. Be still. Let His peace rise within you again.

DAY 35 | WHEN HOPE WON'T LET GO

Scripture:

"Let us hold unswervingly to the hope we profess, for He who promised is faithful."
— Hebrews 10:23 (NIV)

Reflection

There's something about the quiet after Christmas. The lights dim. The wrapping paper's gone. The house feels both full and empty at the same time. For some, it's relief — the chaos is over. But for others, it's a reminder that the thing we prayed for... still hasn't happened yet.

I've had those years — sitting in the stillness after the holidays, reflecting on everything that didn't go as planned. The relationship that ended — or the one that never happened. The job that didn't come through. The dream that feels like it's moving in slow motion. And if I'm honest, there were moments I whispered, "Lord... did You forget about me? Did I do something wrong?"

But even in that quiet ache, something small — something holy — begins to flicker. Hope. Not loud, not flashy, just a gentle glow that refuses to go out. Because hope isn't always a shout; sometimes it's a whisper that says, "He's still faithful."

I've learned that hope doesn't always feel like strength. Sometimes it's just deciding to get up, fix your coffee, and try again. Sometimes it's choosing joy when sadness feels easier. Hope — like joy — is a choice. It's within my control. When I take a step toward it, God meets me there — even if I don't get it perfectly right, He honors my try.

There have been times when I didn't feel hopeful — but that flicker inside me wouldn't die. That's because it's not mine to keep alive; it's His Spirit keeping it lit. Romans 15:13 says He's the God of hope, which means even when mine runs low, He has an endless supply.

So as the decorations get packed away (and y'all, they should be down before Dr. King's birthday — come on now!) and the holiday bustle fades, don't wallow in what wasn't or hasn't happened. Instead, focus on all that has happened — the prayers He answered, the strength you gained, the peace you found — and all that's still yet to come.

If your hope feels small right now — flickering like the last candle in the window — don't despise it. Protect it. Nurture it. Feed it with prayer, worship, and truth. Hope is how your soul breathes when life feels heavy. It's how your faith keeps saying, "Even if not yet, I still believe."

And just like that candlelight on a winter night, your small flame still shines bright enough for God to see.

Meditation

When hope spark, faith fuels it.

You don't have to burn bright to be seen —

even the faintest light matters to God.

Survival Tip – Feed the Flame

When you feel weary, do one thing that reignites your faith —

read a promise, play a worship song, or write down one thing God did do this year.

Focus on His faithfulness, not your frustration.

Connection Challenge

Check on someone who's quietly struggling.

A simple "I see you, and I'm praying for you"

can reignite hope in ways you'll never know.

▌ Song of the Day "My Hope Is Built" – Rev. Timothy Wright

A timeless reminder that even when life shakes, our foundation in Christ never moves.

As the song declares, "My hope is built on nothing less than Jesus' blood and righteousness."

When everything else feels uncertain, this song anchors your heart back to the One who never fails.

▌Bonus Track: "Over and Over" – Trin-i-tee 5:7 & PJ Morton

This song is my reminder that no matter the season, the relationship status, or the emotions we face — God keeps blessing us over and over. Through every high, every heartbreak, every wait, and every win, His faithfulness hasn't wavered.

It's the perfect way to end this devotional soundtrack — a reminder that we don't just survive seasons; we grow through them because His grace keeps pouring, over and over.

> "Even when I didn't see it, He was working. Even when I doubted, He was faithful. Every page, every prayer, every tear — He turned into praise."

FINAL REFLECTION – WHAT THE LONELY DO AT CHRISTMAS

Maybe the truth is, loneliness doesn't always look like tears on Christmas morning or sitting in the dark staring at the tree lights. Sometimes it looks like strength — showing up when no one clapped, cooking dinner for one, buying your own gift, or deciding to find joy anyway.

If anyone ever asks what the lonely do at Christmas, tell them this:

We heal.

We grow.

We laugh again.

We rediscover our worth in the One who never left.

We love ourselves, we lean on Jesus, and we live in expectation of all that's yet to come.

Because the truth is, we're not just surviving this season — we're becoming in it.

We live life, love self, and wait well on God.

Because our best days aren't behind us — they're just ahead. ▎✦

CLOSING PRAYER

Heavenly Father,

Thank You for walking with me through this season — the highs and the lows, the laughter and the lonely moments. Thank You for reminding me that even in my waiting, You are working.

Lord, help me to carry the lessons I've learned here beyond the holidays. When the noise fades and the decorations come down, let my heart remain anchored in hope. When my thoughts start to wander toward what I don't have, bring my focus back to all that I do — peace, purpose, grace, and the promise of Your love.

Remind me that joy isn't a feeling; it's a choice. Help me to keep choosing it — even when it's hard, even when I'm tired, even when I can't see what's next.

And when my faith flickers, breathe on it again.

Surround me with people who speak life. Give me courage to set boundaries that protect my peace. Fill my home and my heart with Your presence — the kind that heals, restores, and overflows.

Lord, I may not have everything I want, but I have everything I need — You.

And because of that, I can face every tomorrow with faith and expectation.

In Jesus' name,

Amen.

A PRAYER FOR YOU

Father,

I lift up the one who is reading this right now. You know their heart, their story, and every silent prayer they've whispered when no one else was listening. I thank You for allowing them to walk through these pages — for every tear, every moment of laughter, every time they chose to hope again even when it was hard.

Lord, remind them that they are not forgotten. When the world feels quiet and the nights feel long, let them sense Your presence wrapping around them like a warm blanket. Remind them that even in their waiting, You are working — and that their story is still being written with purpose, beauty, and grace.

Restore their joy, renew their peace, and refresh their spirit. Help them see themselves the way You see them — whole, loved, and worthy of every good thing You have planned.

As this season comes to an end, let a new season begin — one filled with laughter that reaches their soul, love that reflects Your heart, and faith that keeps them anchored in You.

In Jesus' name,

Amen.

WHAT DO THE LONELY DO AT CHRISTMAS?

Holiday Survival Cheat Sheet

Daily Heart Check

- Write down one gratitude + one grief. Both are real, and both matter.

- Whisper a quick prayer: "Lord, remind me I'm not alone today."

- Ask: Am I waiting for joy to find me, or am I choosing it today?

Practical Activities

- Buy yourself one small gift and wrap it.

- Treat yourself to a seasonal drink or simple joy.

- ▌Watch your favorite holiday movie—even if you've seen it 20 times.

- ▌Schedule a quick check-in with a safe friend.

- ▌Send one encouraging text each week— remind someone else they're not alone.

Body & Soul Care

- ▌Play one uplifting song from the playlist while you get ready.

- ▌▌♀□ Take a short walk or stretch when you get home.

- ▌Go to bed 30 minutes earlier—loneliness feels heavier when you're exhausted.

Cycle Breakers

- ✎· Swap 10 minutes of scrolling for journaling or prayer.

- ▊ Write yourself a letter of hope for the New Year—seal it, open it next December.

- ▊ Volunteer, donate, or do something small for someone in need.

Emergency Toolkit (for the heavy days)

- ▊ Play your "go-to" encouragement song or the "What Do The Lonely Do" Playlist.

- ▊ Text or call your safe person: "I just need you to remind me I'm not alone."

- ▊ Speak this out loud: "I am loved. I am seen. I am not forgotten."

- ▊ If suicidal thoughts come: Call 988 (Suicide & Crisis Lifeline). You are too valuable to fight this alone.

✨Remember: Loneliness doesn't get the final say. Emmanuel—God with us—means you are never truly alone.

▌ WHAT DO THE LONELY DO AT CHRISTMAS

The Soundtrack of Survival – Official Devotional Playlist

Curated by Monica Guthrie Purchase

Music has always been one of God's sweetest ways to reach my heart — to comfort, to convict, and to carry me when words alone couldn't.

Every song in this devotional was chosen intentionally to echo the theme, mood, or message of that day's reflection.

Some songs will make you worship.

Some will make you laugh or cry.

And some will remind you that healing, hope, and wholeness can sound like a melody.

As you journey through these devotionals, take time to listen to each song. Let the lyrics sink in. Let them lift your spirit, stir your memories, and strengthen your faith.

▌

How to Listen

Scan the QR code, click here, or search the song titles on your favorite streaming platform — Spotify, Apple Music, YouTube Music, or Amazon Music.

Use this soundtrack as your companion to lift your spirit, quiet your mind, and help you connect even deeper with each devotional moment.

▌ The Soundtrack of Survival

Day 1 – I Am Light – India.Arie

Day 2 – Do You Hear What I Hear – Whitney Houston

Day 3 – Be Blessed – Yolanda Adams

Day 4 – Heaven Help Us All – Stevie Wonder

Day 5 – Better Than You Left Me – Mickey Guyton

Day 6 – Someday at Christmas – Stevie Wonder

Day 7 – You Know My Name– Tasha Cobbs Leonard

Day 8 – A House Is Not a Home – Luther Vandross

Day 9 – Anointing Fall – Monica Purchase

Day 10 – This Christmas – Donny Hathaway

Day 11 – My Worship – Phil Thompson

Day 12 – Silver & Gold – Kirk Franklin

Day 13 – Be Grateful – Walter Hawkins

Day 14 – Brighter Day – Kirk Franklin

Day 15 – Love's in Need of Love Today – Stevie Wonder

Day 16 – Not Gon' Cry – Mary J. Blige

Day 17 – Ex-Factor – Lauryn Hill

Day 18 – Healed – Donald Lawrence & The Tri-City Singers

Day 19 – Cycles – Jonathan McReynolds

Day 20 – Moving Forward – Israel Houghton

Day 21 – Golden – Jill Scott

Day 22 – My Favorite Things – Luther Vandross

Day 23 – Joy – Whitney Houston & The Georgia Mass Choir

Day 24 – I Was Here – Beyoncé

Day 25 – Optimistic – Sounds of Blackness

Day 26 – Better Days – Le'Andria Johnson

Day 27 – Wanna Be Happy? – Kirk Franklin

Day 28 – Encourage Yourself – Donald Lawrence & The Tri-City Singers

Day 29 – Keep the Faith – Faith Evans

Day 30 – Better – Jessica Reedy

Day 31 – You Waited – Travis Greene

Day 32 – Still – Jonathan McReynolds

Day 33 – Help Me- Tamela Mann

Day 34 – Be Still – Yolanda Adams

Day 35 – My Hope Is Built – Rev. Timothy Wright

BonusTrack- Over and Over- Trinitee 5:7 & PJ Morton

❚ FINAL NOTE FROM MONI

May these songs remind you that even in loneliness, you're never alone — God's melody is always playing over you.

Every lyric, every note, every hum and harmony carries a whisper of His presence.

So whether you're sipping cocoa by the tree, sitting in silence, driving home, or dancing around your kitchen, let this soundtrack be your reminder:

You are seen. You are loved. And your story — just like your song — isn't over yet. ❚❚

ABOUT THE AUTHOR

Monica Lynese Guthrie Purchase is an educator, singer, actress, host, and all-around creative force with a heart for ministry, healing, and hope.

Affectionately known as "Just Moni," she's the host of The Waiting Room Podcast—a space designed for Christian singles, especially those over 40, who are learning to live life, love themselves, and wait well on God. Through her voice, her words, and her laughter, Monica encourages others to see that waiting isn't wasted when it's rooted in faith.

With more than 20 years of experience in education administration and leadership, Monica has dedicated her life to empowering others through teaching, encouragement, and authenticity. But her gifts extend far beyond the classroom. As a gifted vocalist, she has provided background vocals (BGVs) for numerous R&B and gospel artists, including Tony! Toni! Toné!, Case, Heather Headley, Tamela Mann, Fred Hammond, and more.

She currently serves faithfully on New Faith Baptist Church International's Levitical Praise Team and with the Daughters of Judah (DOJ) Choir, as well as performing alongside Darius Brooks and The Tommies Reunion Choir—continuing to use her voice to inspire and uplift others through worship.

A proud member of Alpha Kappa Alpha Sorority, Incorporated®, Monica finds deep purpose in serving her community through sisterhood, scholarship, and service.

She is the proud mother of two sons, Jalen (JT) and Josiah, and loving grandmother to Justice—with another precious grandbaby on the way. She's also the proud daughter of her "senagers," Billy and Brenda Guthrie, and the proud auntie of many amazing nieces and nephews who keep her laughing and grounded.

When she's not writing, singing, or recording, you'll find her sipping coffee, brainstorming creative projects, or cracking jokes with her family and chosen sisters. She also loves helping and aiding her family and friends in whatever way she can—because service, laughter, and love are all part of who she is.

Monica's mission is simple yet powerful:

To encourage and empower others to live life fully, love themselves deeply, and wait well on God—

because their best days aren't behind them, they're just ahead.

✉ JustMoniP@gmail.com

Connect with Monica

📱 Facebook: Monica Guthrie Purchase

📷 Instagram: @MoniLove1908

🎵 TikTok: @MoniLove1908

▶□ YouTube: @TheMoniBrand

www.ingramcontent.com/pod-product-compliance
Lightning Source LLC
Chambersburg PA
CBHW051518120626
46551CB00012B/976